THE BOOK OF
Eagles

Bald Eagles

THE BOOK OF
Eagles

By Helen Roney Sattler

Illustrated by Jean Day Zallinger

Lothrop, Lee & Shepard Books
New York

Dedicated to Alice
with greatest affection

ACKNOWLEDGMENTS

I would like to express my deepest appreciation and thanks to Steve K. Sherrod, director of the George Sutton Avian Research Center, Inc., near Bartlesville, Oklahoma, and his assistant, Alan Jenkins, for reading the complete manuscript and adding many valuable pieces of information, and for checking the drawings for accuracy.

Book design by Sylvia Frezzolini
First Edition

1 2 3 4 5 6 7 8 9 10

LIBRARY OF CONGRESS CATALOGING IN PUBLICATION DATA
Sattler, Helen Roney.   The book of eagles / by Helen Roney Sattler : illustrations by Jean Day Zallinger.
p. cm.   Bibliography: p.   Includes index.   Summary: Discusses the physical characteristics, behavior, and life cycle of eagles and describes many individual species, including the African fish eagle, bald eagle, booted eagle, and harpy eagle.
ISBN 0-688-07021-3.   ISBN 0-688-07022-1 (lib. bdg.)   1. Eagles—Juvenile literature. [1. Eagles.]
I. Zallinger, Jean, ill.   II. Title.   QL696.F32S28   1989   598'.916—dc19
88-38806   CIP   AC

Table of Contents

ONE   Lords of the Skies

Eagles live on every continent in the world except Antarctica. They are found in every kind of habitat from dense tropical forests to treeless plains and subdeserts; from mountains to seashores; and from polar regions to the equator. Throughout the world eagles are referred to as "lords of the skies." They are not the largest, or the fastest, or even the highest-flying birds, but in flight or on the hunt, they are among the most majestic of all birds.

Eagles have lived for millions of years. They patrolled the skies long before humans appeared on earth. In recent years many species of eagle have become threatened with extinction. Some species may already be extinct. Humans are responsible for their demise, and only humans can save those that survive.

The word *eagle* comes from the Latin name *aquila*, which was given to the Golden Eagle by the ancient Romans. Today *eagle* refers to four distinct groups of large, strong, flesh-eating birds. These four groups are not closely related to one another, but they have characteristics in common that earn them the right to be called eagles. For example, all are top predators that hunt during the day and sleep at night. They have no real enemies except humans.

Scientific classification of eagles is difficult. They are *raptors*, which means "birds of prey" and comes from the Latin word meaning "plunderer." They are in the suborder of raptors called *accipiter*, and are members of the *Accipitridae* family. Not every bird in this family, however, is an eagle. The family also includes hawks, kites, and vultures. Not everyone agrees which of the large raptors should be called eagles. However, most scientists agree that there are at least sixty species of eagle around the world. Experts group these species into four types: fish and sea eagles, booted or "true" eagles, harpy or buteonine eagles, and snake or serpent eagles. The glossary lists each of these sixty species of eagle alphabetically by its common name. The chart on pages 32–33 lists the species by type and genus.

BOOTED EAGLES
Aquilavus (extinct)
36,000,000 years ago

FISH AND SEA EAGLES
25,000,000 years ago

7

Very few of the sixty species have been carefully studied because eagles are difficult to study in the wild. They are swift and fly so high it is not easy to follow them. Some species are nearly impossible to observe well enough to make definite conclusions about them. Many live in dense jungles where they are seldom seen; some are so rare they are almost never seen.

Only two species, the Bald Eagle and the Golden Eagle, live in the United States. Although many eagles are quite similar to these two, others are quite different. Eagles vary greatly in size. A female Harpy Eagle may be 3 feet long from the top of the head to the end of the tail and may weigh up to 20 pounds—as much as a large turkey! A female Bald Eagle is also 3 feet long and can weigh up to 15 pounds.

Golden Eagle
(booted or
"true" eagle)

Bald Eagle
(fish eagle)

Harpy Eagle
(harpy or buteonine eagle)

Bateleur
(snake or serpent eagle)

Most eagles, however, are much smaller than the Bald and Harpy Eagles. Fifteen of the species weigh less than 3 pounds. A male Ayre's Hawk-eagle is only 16.5 inches long and weighs as little as 1.5 pounds—smaller than a common crow. All female raptors are larger than the males of their species. Some female eagles are up to one-third bigger.

Eagles also differ greatly in color. Most are some shade of brown or black with varying amounts of white. Many are strikingly marked with bars and splotches.

Eagles are a very old group of birds. Some scientists suggest that eagles descended from primitive, insectivorous (in-sec-TIV-o-rus, insect-eating) kites. They seem to have split into two separate lines of evolution. One group developed into the fish and sea eagles and Old World vultures, while the other evolved into booted eagles, harpy eagles, and snake or serpent eagles.

9

fish eagle

snake eagle

The oldest known eagle was a booted eagle that lived 36,000,000 years ago. The booted or "true" eagles are also the most highly evolved and the largest group of birds called eagles. The Golden Eagle belongs to this group. Most booted eagles look somewhat like the Golden Eagle, differing only in size and coloring. Unlike those of all other eagles, the legs of booted eagles are feathered to the toes, which makes the birds look as if they are wearing trousers. Booted eagles live mainly inland, feeding on birds, small mammals, and carrion (dead animals).

The Bald Eagle is a fish eagle. Fish and sea eagles first appeared on earth about 25,000,000 years ago. Except in size and coloring, they are all similar in appearance. They are large birds, although most are smaller than the Bald Eagle. They live near large bodies of water and feed mainly on fish and water birds. Like all eagles, they have sharp, curved talons for grasping prey, but their toes are especially adapted for fishing. Tiny spikes (or spicules) on the bottoms of their toes help hold slippery prey. Fish and sea eagles have short, bare legs covered with scales. These scales are similar to those of reptiles and develop from buds or follicles just as feathers do.

Harpy or buteonine eagles are the largest and most powerful of the eagles. Not much is known about this group because they live in dense jungles and are very difficult to observe. They prey on large mammals, including monkeys.

The snake or serpent eagles are small to medium-size eagles. They are very specialized (adapted to a very specific way of hunting) and are more closely related to hawks than to other eagles. Their diet consists mainly of reptiles. Most live in tropical areas where snakes can be found easily.

Although each group is distinct and has its own preferred diet, all eagles behave in similar ways. They have basically the same type of hunting equipment and are excellent hunters.

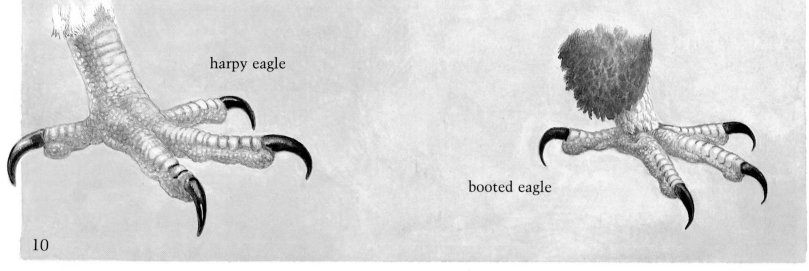

harpy eagle

booted eagle

TWO ✕ Magnificent Hunters

High above its hunting area, a magnificent Golden Eagle soars effort-lessly, searching the ground for prey. Suddenly it swoops, dropping in a swift glide. With the wind whistling through its feathers, it tilts its wings from side to side as it pursues a fleeing chipmunk. Unfor-tunately for the eagle, at the last second the small rodent escapes under a rock.

This is not unusual. Eagles frequently miss their intended prey. First attempts are seldom successful. Nonetheless, eagles rarely go hungry for long, unless prey is scarce. They are superb hunters. De-spite the frequent misses, getting food is so easy for them they often spend only a few hours each day hunting. They are amazingly strong and have wonderful maneuverability in the air.

The slim body of an eagle is quite small and is very lightweight compared to the great spread of the wings. An eagle with a 6-foot wingspan (wing tip to wing tip) may have a body no larger than that of a big chicken. The actual wingspan is known for less than half of the species. Wingspans range from the Little Eagle's slightly more than 3 feet to the 8.5-foot span of a female Martial Eagle.

An eagle's bones are hollow and filled with air, which makes them extremely light. Braces or struts inside give the bones strength. A 14-pound Bald Eagle's bones weigh only a little more than a half pound.

Feathers give an eagle's body a streamlined shape and insulate it from heat and cold without adding excess weight. The 7,000 feathers on a Bald Eagle weigh only 21 ounces—less than 1.5 pounds.

An eagle's wing and tail feathers are incredibly strong. They are made of keratin, the same material as human fingernails. The wing feathers lift and propel the bird. The wings are flatter on the bottom than on top, like the wings of an aircraft. Small feathers called co-verts grow along the forward edges of the wings, making them thicker in front. This causes air to flow faster over the top, providing lift. At the tips of the wings, long feathers called primaries can be spread out like fingers to reduce drag.

Golden Eagle

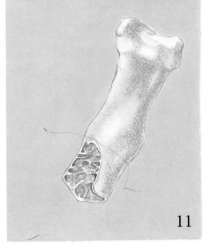

portion of eagle leg bone with interior bracing

Hook and bow barbules
strengthen each wing
and tail feather

secondary
feathers

coverts

primary
feathers

EAGLE WING SECTION

Bald Eagle eye

Nictitating membrane
closes to protect eye

The tail feathers are used for steering and braking. For strength, each wing and tail feather is held together by thousands of tiny hooks and flanges (similar to Velcro) called hook barbules and bow barbules.

The wings of most eagles are long and broad. They are among the most powerful wings on earth, capable of carrying the birds high into the air with little effort and allowing them to swoop down upon prey at incredible speeds. Few eagles have been clocked, but Golden and Bonelli's Eagles sometimes reach speeds of 200 miles per hour in a dive. They normally cruise at about 30 miles per hour. Harpy Eagles can glide among treetops with astonishing agility at 40 to 50 miles per hour.

Eagles are excellent fliers and extremely graceful in the air. To fly, they need plenty of open space and wind flow. When not flapping their wings, they fly somewhat like hang gliders, sometimes using rising hot air currents called thermal updrafts as elevators to rise very high into the sky. At times they soar up to 14,000 feet, so high in the air they cannot be seen from the ground with the naked eye. An eagle may simply spread its wings and float upward on the air current with very little effort. An airborne eagle may be defending its hunting or breeding territory or just soaring for fun. Eagles love to play with the wind. Some hunt on the wing, but most eagles prefer to hunt from a perch, taking to the air only when they cannot find a suitable tree or ledge.

Eagles, like all birds of prey, have excellent hearing. They hunt by sight, however. Their extraordinary eyesight allows them to see both forward and sideways. Their eyes are huge—as large as the eyes of a human in some, though of course their heads are much smaller. Generally, the larger an eye, the farther it can focus and the sharper the vision is. Studies show that the vision of some eagles may be up to seven times as acute as human eyesight. Observers have claimed that a soaring Golden Eagle can see a ground squirrel from 1,000 feet in the air. Even with binoculars, a human could not see so small an animal at that distance. From a soaring position, snake eagles can home in on and catch small, fast-moving, camouflaged snakes in dense jungle.

Once an eagle has spotted its prey, it does not take its eyes off the creature until it strikes. When striking, the eagle plunges, hitting or clutching the prey with its feet. Sometimes an eagle will float slowly down to the prey, dropping out of the sky or tree so silently that the animal doesn't hear it.

Golden Eagle hunting

Bald Eagle

An eagle's feet are deadly weapons. They are equipped with four toes, three in front and one in back. Each toe has a thick, curved, dagger-sharp talon that may be up to 5 inches long. An eagle kills by grasping prey in a viselike grip and piercing it with the long talons.

When eating, the eagle holds the prey with its talons and uses its long, pointed, very powerful, hooked beak to shred and tear the food into bite-sized pieces. Many eagles strip fur or feathers from the catch before shredding and eating the flesh. The beak is almost never used for killing.

As a rule, eagles hunt alone or in pairs, but if there is a great deal of food in one place, many eagles may come together to eat. In Africa, large flocks gather to feast upon grasshoppers or locusts stirred up by the flames of grass fires or to hunt for prey in burned-over areas. Hundreds of Bald Eagles flock along rivers in the Pacific Northwest when hordes of dead salmon fill the streams after spawning. In Alaska, more than one hundred Bald Eagles at a time have fed upon a single beached whale.

Eagles kill only when hungry. Like most predators, they take the easiest meal they can find. Most eagles prefer live food, but many also eat carrion. Some eagles survive on carrion during cold winter months. Certain eagles eat only one kind of food. Others will eat whatever is available. The Tawny Eagle feeds on anything from termites to dead elephants, and even ostrich eggs. Bald Eagles in Alaska sometimes eat garbage. Eagles in northern areas build up fat reserves in their bodies, which they live on when sitting out winter storms.

Most eagles catch their food on the ground or on the surface of water, but some capture birds or snakes in trees and a few catch birds in midair. Some fish eagles are pirates; they hijack other fish-eating birds, such as ospreys, and steal their catch. An eagle, being faster and more powerful than a bird that is carrying a heavy load, may chase the fish-laden bird until it drops its catch. The eagle then plunges after and catches the fish in its talons before it hits the ground.

An eagle's method of hunting varies according to the kind of food it is after. Fish and sea eagles will eat dead fish or waterfowl when they can find them, but are very good at catching live prey when necessary. They usually fly low over the water and snatch surfacing fish or swimming waterfowl with their talons. Sometimes, however, they plunge feet first into the water with a big splash when grabbing their prey. Occasionally a sea eagle will drag a fish to shore if it is too big to carry.

Harpy eagles eat large mammals. They have very strong legs that are as thick as a man's wrist, and hind toes equipped with huge, 5-inch talons. A harpy eagle can drive its talons completely through the body of a sloth or coatimundi. Booted eagles with long toes catch birds on the wing. Booted eagles with small toes and claws catch small mammals.

Tawny Eagles

15

A snake or serpent eagle uses its short, thick toes to grasp thin, wiggling snakes and other reptiles. The bird plunges onto a snake near the head, breaking its neck and paralyzing it. It is thought that the rough scales on their legs may protect snake eagles from venomous snake bites.

Although an eagle's wings are very strong, few eagles attempt to catch prey that weighs more than they do. A carcass too large to carry may be partially eaten on the spot before being taken to the roost or nest.

While all eagles are magnificent hunters, males are especially efficient at catching prey. They are particularly busy during the nesting period. A male must catch food for his mate every day while she is sitting on eggs. He also brings food to the young as long as the eaglets are in the nest.

Brown Snake Eagle

THREE 🦅 Courting and Nesting

During mating season, some eagles spend more time and energy courting than hunting. When male and female Bald Eagles court, they often fly so high that they are barely visible from the ground. They wheel and dip, rising and falling as if on a roller coaster. Occasionally, they come together in the air, then separate. Suddenly one turns over and the two grasp claws. Spreading their wings, they tumble toward the earth, cartwheeling over and over. Just before they reach the ground, they separate again and soar back up into the sky.

Bateleur courtship pose

Not all courtship rituals are this dramatic, but such a performance is typical of the fish and sea eagles. The courtships of almost all eagles begin with a male and female calling to each other, either alone or in duet, from a perch or from high in the air. Forest-dwelling eagles seem to do more calling than those that live in open country. Snake eagles are generally the noisiest. The Crowned Eagle is extremely vocal, while the Martial Eagle is almost silent.

Some eagles do no more than call, but for most species, the main part of the courting ritual takes place in the air. Some perform vigorous undulating, diving, and rolling displays. Bateleurs perform several rolls in quick succession. The display of a Verreaux's Eagle is among the most spectacular. This eagle plunges nearly 1,000 feet, swinging up again at the last minute and looping the loop, or rolling at the top of the upward swoop. Then it swings to and fro as though it were suspended from a pendulum. Each swing may be up to 5,000 feet from beginning to end.

Depending on the species, an eagle may be anywhere from fifteen months to four or five years old before it is mature enough to mate. Mating is usually for life. An eagle takes a new mate only if its first mate dies.

Once paired, the eagles establish a nesting territory, which they fiercely defend against other eagles of the same species and any animal that might be a threat to their young. Eagles return to the same

Bald Eagles cartwheeling

territory year after year. Most eagles require large hunting territories, ranging from less than 25 square miles to 100 square miles or more. The size depends on the terrain, how much food is available, and how many other eagles live nearby.

As soon as the territory is established, the pair begins building a nest. The actual nesting site depends upon the species of eagle. Most eagles prefer peace and quiet when raising a family. They usually build their nests in high, hard-to-reach places such as very tall trees or wide ledges of cliffs. A few species nest on the ground if they live in flat, treeless areas. Fish eagles select sites near water. Many eagles build where there are several very large, tall trees—one for the nest and two or three nearby for lookout posts and landing platforms. The nest is usually built at the top of the tallest tree, 50 to 80 feet above the ground.

The making of the nest, or eyrie (EYE-ry), is hard work and takes a long time—anywhere from several weeks to several months, depending upon the species and the material used. Both eagles labor at this task. The female does most of the actual construction, but both male and female gather the building material. The nest is usually made of twigs and large sticks, some as big around as a man's wrist and up to 5 feet long. An eagle will pick these off the ground or break them from trees by hitting a branch with the full force of its body while grabbing the branch with the talons. Where sticks can't be found, eagles use other material. In the treeless Aleutian Islands near southwestern Alaska, Bald Eagles build nests of seaweed.

The female arranges and works the sticks into an enormous, cuplike nest. She lines the cup with soft material such as grass, leaves, or moss. When the nest is complete, the eagles sometimes collect live evergreen sprigs and insert them into the wall of the nesting cup.

The eagles continue to bring fresh green sprigs throughout the nesting period. No one knows why they do this. Some scientists suggest it is for sanitation. Perhaps the resin from the sprigs prevents the nest from being infested by parasites. Others suggest that the sprigs are used to show that the nest is occupied. Since they can be seen easily by humans, they must be easy for other eagles to see. Still others think the sprigs are simply for decoration. It is possible that they have more than one purpose.

Golden Eagles building a nest

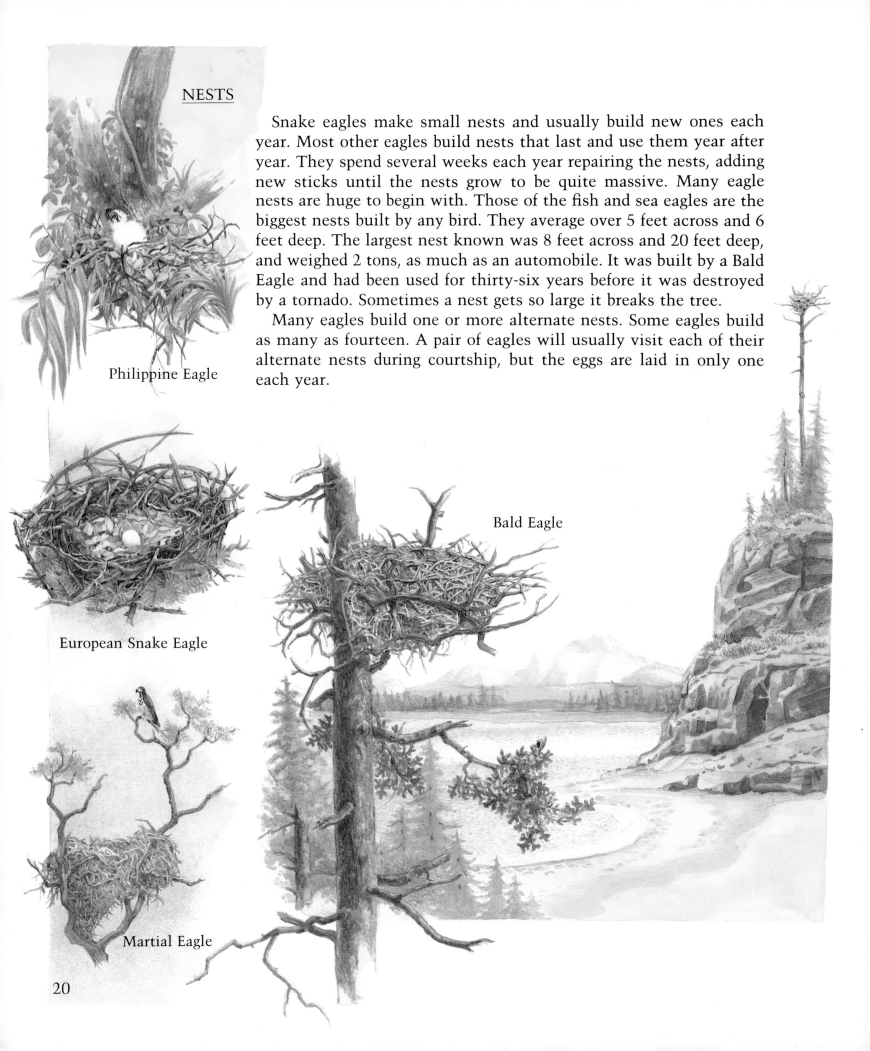

NESTS

Snake eagles make small nests and usually build new ones each year. Most other eagles build nests that last and use them year after year. They spend several weeks each year repairing the nests, adding new sticks until the nests grow to be quite massive. Many eagle nests are huge to begin with. Those of the fish and sea eagles are the biggest nests built by any bird. They average over 5 feet across and 6 feet deep. The largest nest known was 8 feet across and 20 feet deep, and weighed 2 tons, as much as an automobile. It was built by a Bald Eagle and had been used for thirty-six years before it was destroyed by a tornado. Sometimes a nest gets so large it breaks the tree.

Many eagles build one or more alternate nests. Some eagles build as many as fourteen. A pair of eagles will usually visit each of their alternate nests during courtship, but the eggs are laid in only one each year.

Philippine Eagle

European Snake Eagle

Bald Eagle

Martial Eagle

FOUR  Baby Eagles

Female eagles begin laying eggs soon after the nest is built or repaired. Most lay two eggs, but some lay up to four. Others lay only one.

All eagle eggs are large. The smallest is no smaller than a chicken egg. A Bald Eagle's eggs are the size of goose eggs. The largest—those of Harpy, Verreaux's, and Golden Eagles—are as big as the plastic egg used to package some pantyhose. Eagle eggs also vary in shape, texture, and color. Some have rough surfaces, others are smooth. Most are white, but some are mottled or splotched with brown, lilac, or red. The shells are very thick and some are blue on the inside.

The eggs are deposited in the nest two to four days apart. As soon as the first egg is laid, the female begins incubating, or sitting on it, to keep it warm. The incubation period can be rather long, from 33 to 45 days in larger species. Sometimes only the female incubates the eggs, but in most species, the male takes a turn while the female eats and takes a break. The male's main jobs during the incubation period are patrolling the territory, protecting the nest, and providing food for his mate.

Some eagles are quite vicious when defending their nests. They strike out at lightning speed, grabbing and disabling an intruder with their feet. They have killed dogs that were too close to their nests.

Near hatching time, a female will not leave her nest unless she is in great danger. If threatened while sitting on the nest, she spreads her wings, raises the feathers on her head, opens her beak, and rears back on her tail to free her feet. She is clearly saying, "Come closer, and I will clobber you." Few creatures will risk an encounter with those deadly claws. A male eagle warns off intruders by throwing his head back, screaming, and flying toward them with slow, steady wingbeats.

An eagle chick announces that it is ready to hatch by calling from inside the egg. It then pecks a hole in the egg with its "egg tooth"—

EGGS

Golden Eagle

Imperial Eagle

Bald Eagle

Tawny Eagle

Bonelli's Eagle

21

Bald Eagle egg

egg in nest

a small spur that every baby bird has near the tip of its beak. The wedge-shaped crystals in the shell of the egg, arranged like the stones in an arch, make the egg strong and hard to break from the outside, but easy to break from the inside. Nonetheless, it takes an eaglet about fifteen hours to peck the first hole in the thick shell. It may take another thirty-five to forty hours to break out of the shell completely.

When born, an eaglet is covered with a fine down, which may be white, gray, buff, or brown. Baby eagles are quite ugly and small considering the size of their eggs—Bald Eagles weigh only 3 ounces at birth. Newborn eaglets are too weak and helpless to stand. Their heads are much too big for their scrawny bodies, and they can't hold them up for long. The effort of breaking out of the egg completely exhausts them.

It takes several hours for the exhausted chicks to recover and for their down to dry. For the first week the parents brood the chicks almost constantly. That is, they keep the eaglets warm or shade them from the sun. Sometimes the father broods while the mother eats, but mostly he hunts. He brings prey back to the nest for both the young and the mother. With her hooked beak, the mother tears the food into tiny shreds and feeds it to the eaglets.

Young eaglets have enormous appetites. They eat almost as much food as adult eagles, and they grow rapidly. At four weeks they may

male Bald Eagle

female Bald Eagle
incubating eggs

Bald Eagle
chicks

be eleven times larger than at hatching. At six weeks they may weigh forty times as much!

By the time they are three weeks old, most eaglets have lost their first soft down and have grown a second, thicker, and woolier coat. This coat is usually the same color as the first, but may be a little lighter or darker.

Now the eaglets become more active. They move about the nest on their ankles and stumplike wings. By five weeks feathers begin replacing down on the wings and tails. Their beaks, talons, and heads are almost completely mature. They are still incredibly unattractive, but they can now stand and waddle. They defecate outside the nest, balancing on the rim with outstretched wings. They can also feed on prey dropped into the nest. At this time the mother joins the male in hunting, and both parents guard the nest.

The first egg laid is the first hatched, so the last eaglet may be two or three days younger than the first one. The younger eaglet is usually smaller and weaker than the firstborn, and the stronger eaglet grabs most of the food. Second-born eaglets often die of starvation once they begin feeding themselves, especially if food is scarce. Among some booted eagles the stronger eaglet often attacks and kills its nest mate, regardless of how much food is available. Scientists call this the "Cain and Abel battle."

Most eaglets have full juvenile plumage by the time they are nine

fledgling Bald Eagle

female Bald Eagle feeding chick

immature
Tawny Eagle

immature
Harpy Eagle

immature
Imperial Eagle

weeks old, although for some this feathering takes three months. Bald Eagles are completely feathered at eight weeks of age. Even though feathered juveniles are almost as large as adults, they usually don't look much like their parents. The majority are brown or brown with white markings. The young of many species of eagle look very much alike, and sometimes it is difficult to tell the young of one species from those of another. Most eagles are four or five years old before they have adult plumage. Young Bateleurs do not look like their parents until they are seven or eight years old.

Once they are feathered, the young spend a great deal of time preening, or cleaning their feathers, and exercising. They practice seizing objects and attacking food with their feet. Some pick up sticks and other articles they find in the nest. An eaglet may toss an object into the air or prance around the nest holding it in one foot or in its beak. Or two chicks may play tug-of-war. Eaglets exercise their wing muscles by perching on the rim of the nest and flapping their wings. Sometimes they become airborne and hover over the nest. Occasionally an updraft of wind lifts a young eaglet into the air. An eaglet that is blown to the ground before it can fly could be doomed. The parents will answer its distress call, but if it has landed in dense vegetation they may not be able to reach it. If the eaglet can flop into an open area, the parents will feed it, but it may be in great danger from predators.

After practicing flying many times, eaglets may hop from the nest to a nearby branch in the nesting tree or to another part of the cliff ledge. These excursions are usually short and the eaglets soon return to the nest.

Most fledgling eaglets are two to four months old, depending upon their species, and have reached their full adult size before they try to fly. The largest eagles take longest to begin flying, and tropical species usually take longer than species in temperate climates. Verreaux's Eagles fly at 90 to 95 days of age, while Golden and Bald Eagles leave the nest at between 65 and 85 days.

An eaglet's first flight is more like a glide than real flying. The flight is often short, though it can be to a tree a mile or more away. This is a critical time for an eaglet. If it misses the top branches and lands too low, it may have difficulty taking off again. The eaglet must have plenty of clearance for its long wings. Good coordination is required for landing on the top branches. It may take several days or weeks before an eaglet can fly well. Its quills are still growing and are not yet firm.

Tawny Eagles:
male (left), female (right)

Even after becoming accomplished fliers, eaglets of many species return to the nests or nest trees to spend the night or to eat. The nests now serve as dining tables as the parents continue to bring food and the eaglets continue to take their meals there. Soon the eaglets will fly up to take prey from a parent bringing food to the nest.

As the eaglets grow older, they accompany their parents on longer and longer flights from the nest. Finally they are not fed near the nest at all. By six months most eaglets are skilled fliers. In general, young eagles continue to depend upon their parents for food for some time after leaving the nest. They stay with their parents until they have mastered their hunting skills. Sometimes the skills are strengthened through games, such as dropping sticks and catching them in midair. Although some eaglets are dependent for up to eleven months, they are usually skillful hunters about two months after the first flight.

Once they have learned to kill for themselves, eaglets are totally independent and usually fly off on their own. Species in colder climates usually migrate to warmer regions in the fall. Some tropical or subtropical species migrate to cooler areas in summer. Juveniles often migrate before the adults. Young eagles are somewhat nomadic, wandering in search of adequate food supplies. When eagles mature, they almost always return to their hatching area to mate and establish a nesting territory.

The period immediately after independence is perhaps the most dangerous time for young eagles. If they survive their first year, they may live for quite a long time. Some eagles live twenty years or more in the wild. Bateleurs have lived forty years in captivity.

26

immature White Sea Eagle

FIVE ❧ Humans: Friends or Foes?

It was feeding time at the George Sutton Avian Research Center near Bartlesville, Oklahoma. A scientist pulled an eagle-head puppet over her hand and placed a shred of meat in its beak. Then, making as little noise as possible, she pushed the puppet through a small door above the nest of a two-week-old baby Bald Eagle. The eaglet eagerly grabbed the meat and swallowed it.

The scientist is part of a program that is attempting to increase the number of Bald Eagles and to restore nesting populations to former nesting areas throughout the United States. She uses the puppet to prevent direct human contact with the young birds so that they will remain wild.

Bald Eagles in Louisiana and Florida lay eggs from November through January. If their eggs are destroyed or disappear early during this period, they will lay another clutch (set of eggs). These scientists are taking advantage of this behavior. They remove eggs laid in November, causing the birds to lay a second clutch. The first clutch is taken to the research center and placed in incubators. After they hatch, the eaglets are settled in nestlike tubs located in glass-enclosed, temperature-controlled rooms. When the eaglets are eight weeks old, they are "hacked," or placed in outdoor nests atop wooden towers located in wildlife refuges. For protection, the nests are built inside barred cages. Scientists drop food into the nests every day. The bars are removed from the cages when the eaglets are ready to fly at eleven weeks. The scientists continue to feed the eaglets, however, until they are old enough to fend for themselves. It is hoped that the eagles will remain in the area where they are released and establish a nesting territory there when they mature.

This is one of many programs throughout the world that are designed to help prevent the extinction of eagles. In Spain and other places in Europe, scientists remove the second-hatched chicks of Lesser Spotted and Imperial Eagles from their nests. Some are placed in the

Bald Eagle chick

collecting
eggs from nest

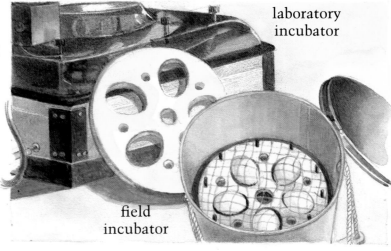
laboratory
incubator

field
incubator

newly hatched chick

feeding chick,
using rubber eagle puppet

banding a young eagle

nests of Black Kites. They are returned to their own nests when the danger of being killed by their nest mates has passed.

Eagles have few enemies besides humans. Natural causes such as disease, severe weather, and starvation when prey is scarce have kept their population in control. Also, animals including crows, raccoons, and snakes eat eggs and eaglets. The number of eagles remained about the same for centuries. In the twentieth century their numbers began to decrease. There are now less than half as many eagles in the world as there were one hundred years ago. Many species are in grave danger of disappearing completely. Some eagles are already so rare that it is extremely unusual to see one.

Humans are to blame for this. By moving into wilderness areas, cutting trees, and clearing the land, they have destroyed the habitats of many eagles. Some species of eagle adapt to the presence of humans, but most don't. Most will not nest or hunt in areas occupied by humans.

Many countries are trying to protect eagles. In the United States, millions of acres of land have been set aside as sanctuaries for Bald Eagles and Golden Eagles. In Ethiopia, eucalyptus trees have been planted on grassy, treeless plateaus to provide nesting places for Tawny Eagles. Other countries have begun similar projects, but more needs to be done.

Another man-made problem for eagles is contaminated food. Farmers use poisons to kill insects and weeds. Factories spew chemicals that pollute air and water. Small animals and fish absorb the poisons. When eagles eat the contaminated animals and fish, they too are poisoned. Eagles have died of lead poisoning after eating ducks wounded with lead pellets from hunters' shotguns. Some have been poisoned by bait set for coyotes and other animals. Many countries have passed laws to control pollution and the use of poisons. DDT, an insecticide that causes eagles' eggshells to become so thin they break in the nest, has been banned for most uses in the United States since 1970. However, DDT can last in the environment for over twenty years. It still occurs in some legal pesticides, and it is still a legal product in many countries of the world.

Sheep farmers throughout the world once shot thousands of eagles because they believed the birds killed their lambs. Actually, eagles eat very few lambs, and most of those are dead when the eagles find them. Although eagles provide a very valuable service to farmers by killing millions of rodents, sportsmen once shot them because they occasionally killed game birds. Today, many places throughout the

raccoon devouring
eagle egg

measuring
eggshell thickness

world have laws against shooting an eagle. In the United States, the first offense of harming a Bald or Golden Eagle or disturbing the nests, eggs, or eaglets can result in a fine of up to $5,000 or one year in prison.

Accidents kill many eagles. Large eagles often use power-line poles for lookout posts. Many have been electrocuted when their long wings touched two wires at once, completing an electric circuit. Some power companies now put barriers on the most dangerous spots to keep the birds from landing or perching on them. Some companies have also started building nesting platforms on power towers that are located in flat, open country where there is plenty of food, but few trees for nesting.

The United States government grants special licenses to people who care for sick or injured eagles in their homes. Eagles that recover completely are released. An injured eagle that can no longer hunt for prey can be kept for breeding. Eaglets born in captivity are placed in the nests of wild eagles or released by the hacking method. Most adult eagles are enthusiastic parents and readily accept and rear foster chicks. Sometimes unreleasable eagles are brought to schools as part of a program to give children a better understanding of these magnificent birds and their problems.

To ensure the survival of the world's eagles, scientists must learn more about the birds and their needs. This is very interesting work, but it is sometimes dangerous and also expensive. The general public, including many schoolchildren, are assisting by donating money to help finance this research.

Some of the money goes to help pay for banding eaglets. Banding helps scientists learn where eaglets go after leaving the nest. Biologists fasten numbered bands to the chicks' legs and keep track of them as they grow up. Others strap transmitters to the backs of fledglings and track them with satellites. Using airplanes, scientists also locate and count the number of eagle nests, eggs, and eaglets in a specific area to determine the level of the population.

the injured eagle
at the Bronx Zoo

30

the hack tower used by
George Miksch Sutton
Avian Research Center

Studying eagles is difficult because they are hard to track after they begin flying. It is easiest to study them in the nest, but that can be dangerous. A scientist may be attacked by adult eagles while climbing a tall tree or cliff to remove eggs or chicks or to band an eaglet. Scientists who do this kind of work, however, are dedicated and think that what they are learning makes it worth the risks.

We now know the causes of many of the problems that threaten eagles. Most of them were created by humans and can be solved. It is our responsibility to find the solutions. Without man-made threats, eagles can take care of themselves very well. Our skies and our lives would be poorer without the presence of the majestic birds called eagles.

Eagles Listed by Groups and Genera

Scientists group all living things according to their similarities and relationships. They give each a two-part scientific name using Greek or Latin words. The first word names the genus and the second word the species. This name is used by scientists throughout the world. It prevents the confusion caused when two unrelated species are called by the same common name in different regions.

The chart below shows the relationships of eagles. It lists them by groups and genera, using their common names.

In the glossary, each eagle is listed alphabetically by its common name followed by its scientific name.

BOOTED OR "TRUE" EAGLES

GENUS *Aquila*
- Golden Eagle
- Greater Spotted Eagle
- Gurney's Eagle
- Imperial Eagle
- Lesser Spotted Eagle
- Tawny Eagle
- Verreaux's Eagle
- Wahlberg's Eagle
- Wedge-tailed Eagle

GENUS *Hieraaetus*
- African Hawk-eagle
- Ayres' Hawk-eagle
- Bonelli's Eagle
- Booted Eagle
- Chestnut-bellied Hawk-eagle
- Little Eagle

GENUS *Ictinaetus*
- Indian Black Eagle

GENUS *Lophaetus*
- Long-crested Eagle

GENUS *Oroaetus*
- Isidor's Eagle

GENUS *Polemaetus*
- Martial Eagle

GENUS *Spizaetus*
- Black Hawk-eagle
- Blyth's Hawk-eagle
- Cassin's Hawk-eagle
- Celebes Hawk-eagle
- Crested Hawk-eagle
- Java Hawk-eagle
- Mountain Hawk-eagle
- Ornate Hawk-eagle
- Philippine Hawk-eagle
- Wallace's Hawk-eagle

GENUS *Spizastur*
- Black and White Hawk-eagle

GENUS *Stephanoaetus*
- Crowned Eagle

FISH AND SEA EAGLES

GENUS *Gypohierax*
   Vulturine Fish Eagle

GENUS *Haliaeetus*
   African Fish Eagle
   Bald Eagle
   Madagascar Fish Eagle
   Pallas' Sea Eagle
   Sandford's Sea Eagle
   Steller's Sea Eagle
   White-bellied Sea Eagle
   White-tailed Sea Eagle

GENUS *Ichthyophaga*
   Gray-headed Fishing Eagle
   Lesser Fishing Eagle

HARPY OR BUTEONINE EAGLES

GENUS *Harpia*
   Harpy Eagle

GENUS *Harpyhaliaetus*
   Black Solitary Eagle
   Crowned Solitary Eagle

GENUS *Harpyopsis*
   New Guinea Harpy Eagle

GENUS *Morphnus*
   Guiana Crested Eagle

GENUS *Pithecophaga*
   Philippine Eagle

SNAKE OR SERPENT EAGLES

GENUS *Circaetus*
   Brown Snake Eagle
   European Snake Eagle
   Smaller Banded Snake Eagle
   Southern Banded Snake Eagle

GENUS *Dryotriorchis*
   Congo Serpent Eagle

GENUS *Eutriorchis*
   Madagascar Serpent Eagle

GENUS *Spilornis*
   Andaman Serpent Eagle
   Celebes Serpent Eagle
   Crested Serpent Eagle
   Nicobar Serpent Eagle
   Philippine Serpent Eagle

GENUS *Terathopius*
   Bateleur

Glossary of Eagles

Each eagle's range of habitation is shown by green area on map.

African Fish Eagle

(Haliaeetus vocifer) This white, chestnut, and black fish eagle is one of the best-known eagles. Males weigh 4.3 to 5.5 pounds; females weigh up to 8 pounds. It lives along shores throughout Africa south of the Sahara Desert. It eats fish that swim near the surface, flamingos, and young waterfowl. When courting, it soars alone or in pairs, calling a loud, clear, "Weeah, hyo-hyo-hyo." Its eggs are incubated for about 45 days. Its young fly by 75 days after hatching.

African Hawk-eagle

(Hieraaetus spilogaster) This booted eagle is closely related to Bonelli's Eagle. Males weigh 2.5 to 3 pounds; females weigh 3 to 3.8 pounds. Adults are black and white; juveniles are dark brown and rust. It lives in woodlands of southern Africa. It soars in courtship, whistling a mellow, fluting, "Kla-klu, klu, kluee." Its one to three sparingly marked eggs are incubated for about 44 days. Fledglings fly by 70 days of age. Its numbers are decreasing.

American Eagle—*See* Bald Eagle.

AFRICA

wingspan 6.3–7.75 ft
underside

underside

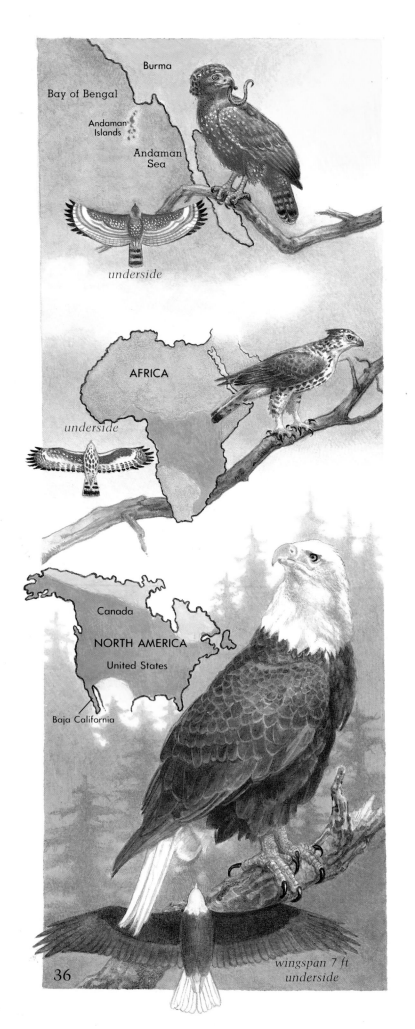

Andaman Serpent Eagle

(*Spilornis elgini*) Almost nothing is known about this 22-inch, white-spotted, brown snake eagle. Fewer than 100 are known to exist. It lives in clearings of tropical forests on the Andaman Islands in the Bay of Bengal.

Ayres' Hawk-eagle

(*Hieraaetus ayresii*) This 16.5- to 19-inch booted eagle is one of the smallest eagles. Males weigh 1.6 pounds; females weigh about 2 pounds. This rare eagle lives in the tropical forests of Africa and eats birds. Adults are brown and white; juveniles are dark brown and buff. In courtship, pairs whistle a high-pitched, melodious, "Hueeeep hueeeep," while diving. Their sparsely blotched, single egg is incubated for 45 days. The young fly within 75 days of hatching.

Bald Eagle

(*Haliaeetus leucocephalus*) Also called American Eagle. This fish eagle is the only eagle with a white head and tail. It lives in North America along seacoasts, lakes, and rivers from Alaska south to Florida and Baja California, Mexico. It is 29 to 36 inches long and weighs from 6 to 15 pounds. Bald Eagles that live in the north migrate to warmer regions in winter. They are larger than those that live all year in the South. Bald Eagles eat fish, waterfowl, rabbits, and sometimes carrion. Their spectacular aerial acrobatics during courtship are accompanied by a squeaky, cackling, "Kar, kar, kar." Their eggs are incubated 35 days. Young fly by 75 days after hatching. The distribution of this eagle is greatly reduced in much of its former range.

Bateleur

(Terathopius ecaudatus) This 24-inch, beautifully colored snake eagle is one of the most magnificent birds of Africa. It has long, broad wings and a very short tail. Males weigh 4 to 6.5 pounds; females weigh slightly more. Bateleurs are quite common in tropical grasslands of Africa, but their numbers are decreasing. They eat snakes, insects, fish, mammals, and birds, sometimes pirating food from other birds. Their courtship ritual includes spectacular dives, chases, talon clasps, and rollovers. Normally silent, they call a loud, harsh, "Schaaaaaaw," in courtship. They incubate their single egg for about 52 days and their young fly 110 to 115 days after hatching.

Beaudouin's Harrier Eagle—A subspecies of the European Snake Eagle.

Black and Chestnut Eagle—*See* Isidor's Eagle.

Black and White Hawk-eagle

(Spizastur melanoleucus) Very little is known about this small, 19- to 20-inch booted eagle. Females weigh about 1.7 pounds. Males are smaller. Adults are black and white. Juveniles are similarly colored but have more white markings. This rare eagle lives in tropical jungles of southeastern Mexico and South America. Its eggs have dark brown spots.

Black-Breasted Harrier Eagle—A subspecies of the European Snake Eagle.

Black Eagle—*See* Verreaux's Eagle.

AFRICA

underside (male)

wingspan 5.8 ft

underside (female)

Central America

SOUTH AMERICA

underside

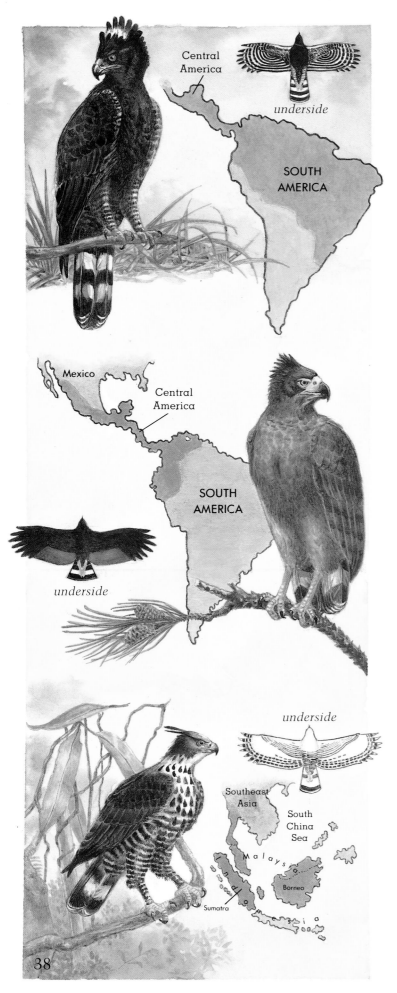

Black Hawk-eagle

(Spizaetus tyrannus) This 23- to 26-inch booted eagle has barred wings and tail and a short, broad crest on its head. Juveniles have brown backs and streaked undersides. Males weigh 2 pounds; females 2.5 pounds. This eagle is fairly common in tropical forested lowlands of Central America and northern South America. It probably eats birds and smaller mammals. This eagle is quite noisy during courtship. It gives a loud, ringing, even-pitched, "Ker ker, ker ker, cu-wu'er," while soaring. It builds its nest in clumps of palm trees.

Black Solitary Eagle

(Harpyhaliaetus solitarius) This rare, 24- to 26-inch, slate-gray-and-white harpy eagle lives in tropical mountain forests of Mexico and northern South America. It probably eats snakes and medium-size mammals. This noisy bird calls, "Yeep-yeep-yeep-yeep-yeep-yeep," or "Pu-pu-pu-pu-pu," when excited.

Blyth's Hawk-eagle

(Spizaetus alboniger) This handsome, 19- to 21-inch booted eagle is not well known. It lives in tropical mountain forests of Southeast Asia and eats tree-dwelling mammals, birds, and bats. It has a 2-inch crest consisting of two or three feathers. Adults are black and white; juveniles are brown with black bars on their tails. It utters a shrill scream while soaring.

Bonelli's Eagle

(Hieraaetus fasciatus) This slim, 26- to 29-inch booted eagle is an aggressive hunter that eats birds and mammals. Males weigh 3.7 to 4.4 pounds; females weigh 5.25 to 5.5 pounds. Adults are dark brown and white; juveniles are brown with rust-colored heads. This eagle lives in wooded, rocky mountains of Europe, Asia, and Africa. It usually nests on cliffs. It is silent, except in courtship, when it gives a low-pitched, fluting, "Klu-klu, klu-klu," cry while circling, undulating, and plunging. Its two spotted and streaked eggs are incubated for 40 days. Its young fly about 65 days after hatching.

Booted Eagle

(Hieraaetus pennatus) This very small booted eagle is 18 to 21 inches long. Adults are dark brown to black on top and white underneath. Juveniles look similar but have rust-colored undersides with dark streaks. Males weigh 1 to 1.7 pounds; females weigh 1.8 to 2.75 pounds. They live in high, mountainous woodlands of southern Europe, Africa, and Asia. They eat small birds, small mammals, and lizards. Their courtship ritual is a series of dives accompanied by a high-pitched, shrill whistle, "Ki-kee," or "Pi-peee, pi-pi-pi-pi-peee." Their two brown-spotted eggs are incubated for 38 days. The young fly by 8 weeks after hatching.

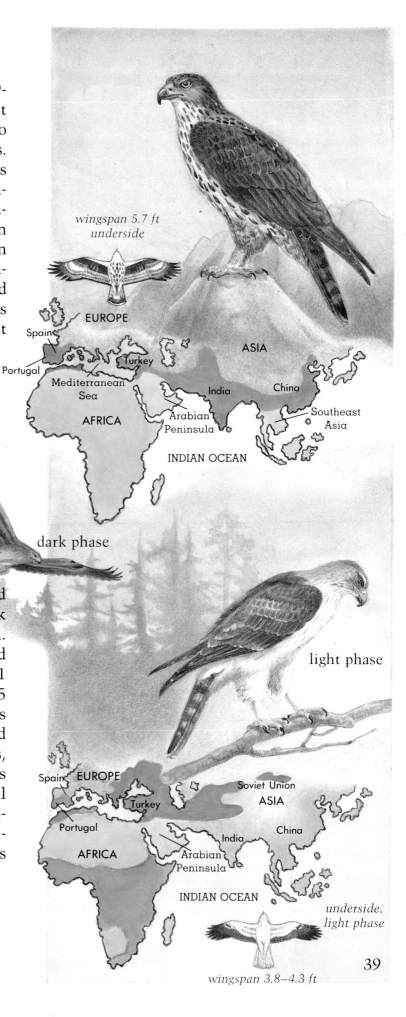

wingspan 5.7 ft
underside

EUROPE
Spain
Portugal
Mediterranean Sea
Turkey
AFRICA
ASIA
India
China
Arabian Peninsula
Southeast Asia
INDIAN OCEAN

dark phase

light phase

Spain EUROPE
Portugal
Turkey
AFRICA
Soviet Union
ASIA
India
China
Arabian Peninsula
INDIAN OCEAN

underside, light phase

39

wingspan 3.8–4.3 ft

Wahlberg's Eagle

wingspan 6.56 ft
underside

AFRICA

BOOTED OR "TRUE" EAGLES

This is the most evolved group of eagles. Though found throughout the world, they are most abundant in Europe, Asia, and Africa. They live inland and feed on birds, small mammals, and carrion. They range from 16 to 36 inches in length and weigh 1 to 14 pounds. Most are black or some shade of brown. Many are strikingly marked with bars and streaks. Most have long tails and long, broad wings, but the hawk-eagles have shorter wings and longer tails than the others in the group. Booted eagles lay one to three eggs. Their large nests measure 2 to 10 feet across and 1 to 12 feet deep. They are usually built in trees, though sometimes on cliffs. Hatchlings are nearly always white and, in some genera, the firstborn often kills the second-born.

The 9 genera of booted eagles are *Aquila, Hieraaetus, Ictinaetus, Lophaetus, Oroaetus, Polemaetus, Spizaetus, Spizastur,* and *Stephanoaetus.* There are 31 species of booted eagles.

Brown Harrier Eagle—*See* Brown Snake Eagle.

Brown Snake Eagle

(Circaetus cinereus) Also called Brown Harrier Eagle. This dark gray-brown snake eagle spends most of its time perched. It is 25 inches long and weighs 3.4 to 5.4 pounds. It lives in dry woodlands of Africa and eats snakes, including cobras. This eagle soars in courtship, calling a raucous, "Kok-kok-kok-kaaaw." Its egg is incubated about 50 days. Its young fly by 110 days after hatching.

Cassin's Hawk-eagle

(Spizaetus africanus) We have very little knowledge of this small, 21-inch booted eagle. It is very rare and lives in dense tropical rain forests of west Africa, where it is usually seen soaring above the forest canopy. Adults are gray-brown and white; juveniles are much paler with red-brown heads and cinnamon-colored breasts. Males weigh 2 to 2.3 pounds; females weigh 2.5 pounds. It eats birds and squirrels. Its call is a high, clear scream, "Wheeee-e."

Celebes Hawk-eagle

(Spizaetus lanceolatus) Little is known about this small, 22-inch booted eagle. It lives in dense tropical forests of Sulawesi (formerly Celebes Island) in Indonesia. This rare, dark-brown-and-rust bird has a pointed crown. Juveniles have white heads, brown backs, and white undersides. Scientists think it eats birds.

Celebes Serpent Eagle

(Spilornis rufipectus) This 19-inch, dark-brown snake eagle is very rare. It lives in the tropical savannas of Sulawesi (formerly Celebes Island), and Sula Islands of Indonesia. It eats lizards, small snakes, and rodents.

AFRICA

underside

Borneo

Sulawesi

INDIAN OCEAN

Sulawesi

Sula Islands

underside

41

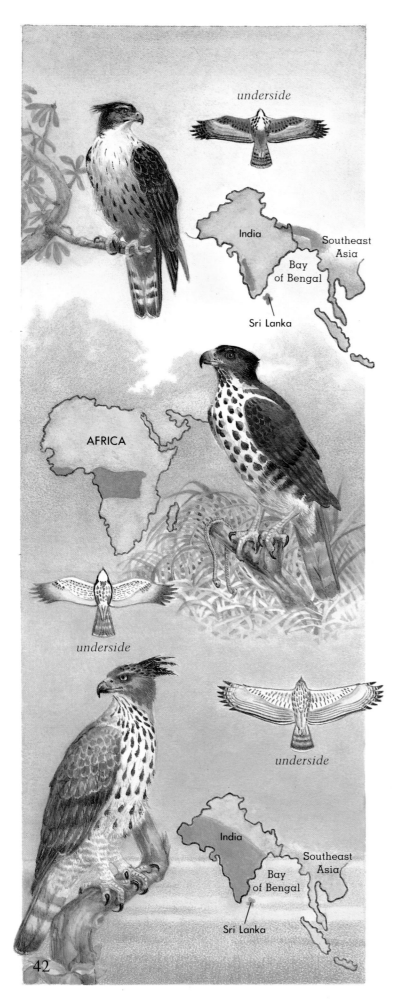

underside

India

Southeast Asia

Bay of Bengal

Sri Lanka

AFRICA

underside

underside

India

Southeast Asia

Bay of Bengal

Sri Lanka

Changeable Hawk-eagle—*See* Crested Hawk-eagle.

Chestnut-bellied Hawk-eagle

(Hieraaetus kienerii) Also called Rufous-bellied Eagle. This 17- to 20-inch booted eagle lives in forests and open hillsides of southern Asia. Adults are black, white, and chestnut, with short crests on their heads; juveniles are mottled brown and white. They eat large birds. This is a very silent bird and its call is unknown. Both parents incubate the single egg, which is white with red, brown, or gray blotches.

Congo Serpent Eagle

(Dryotriorchis spectabilis) This 21.5- to 23-inch, dark-brown-and-white snake eagle is little known. It lives in dense rain forests of equatorial Africa and eats snakes, lizards, and toads. It is seldom seen, except when uttering a mournful, "Cow, cow, cow, cow," or a catlike meow from a perch.

Crested Hawk-eagle

(Spizaetus cirrhatus) Also called Changeable Hawk-eagle. This slim, 20- to 24-inch booted eagle has a long, floppy, black crest. Adults are brown and some have white undersides streaked with black. Juveniles are much paler, with fawn-colored heads and white undersides. Females weigh about 3 pounds; males are smaller. They live in tropical savannas and forests of southern Asia. They eat mammals and lizards. During mating season, they soar while screaming a ringing, "Kleee-klee-ek." Their single egg has pink specks.

Crested Serpent Eagle

(Spilornis cheela) This 24-inch, beautifully marked snake eagle has many subspecies. Most are dark brown and cinnamon colored with white speckles and a black crest. Males weigh about 2 pounds, females weigh slightly more. They live in the tropical woodlands of Asia, the Philippines, and Indonesia. They eat reptiles, tree snakes, and lizards. In courtship, they soar and dive, noisily calling a series of short, low-pitched notes followed by a loud, higher-pitched descending scream. The egg is incubated for 35 days. The young fly by 60 days of age.

Crowned Eagle

(Stephanoaetus coronatus) This beautifully barred, impressively crested booted eagle is one of the most powerful birds on earth. It is 27 to 30 inches long. Males weigh about 8 pounds; females weigh 8 to 9 pounds. Adults are black and cinnamon colored; juveniles are light brown on top and white underneath. It lives in heavily wooded areas in southern Africa and eats large mammals up to two times its own weight. It is very noisy during courtship. The male dives, circles, performs figure eights, and grasps the female's claws while shrieking, "Kewick, kewick, kewick." Its two white eggs hatch in 49 days. Its young fly about 115 days later.

Crowned Solitary Eagle

(Harpyhaliaetus coronatus) This 25- to 27-inch, ashy-brown harpy eagle has a long crest of three or four feathers. It lives in woodlands and savannas of central South America. Although this bird is rather sluggish and quite tame, little is known about it. It seems to eat skunks and other slow-moving mammals.

underside

wingspan 6.5 ft
underside

underside

43

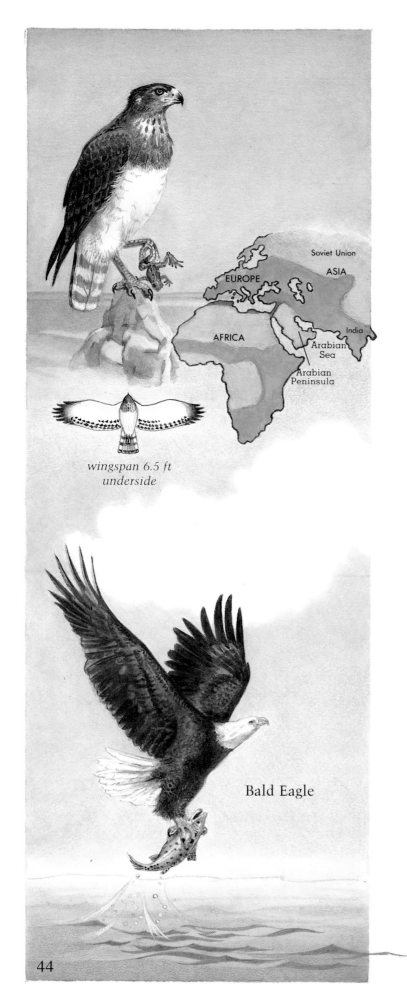

wingspan 6.5 ft
underside

Bald Eagle

European Snake Eagle

(Circaetus gallicus) Also called Serpent Eagle and Short-toed Eagle. Beaudouin's Harrier Eagle and the Black-breasted Harrier Eagle are now considered subspecies of this eagle. These gray-brown and white snake eagles prefer open grasslands in southern and central Europe and Asia. Northern populations migrate to Africa and India in winter. They eat snakes (including venomous species), frogs, rats, birds, and insects. They are 24 to 27 inches long. Males weigh 4 to 4.4 pounds; females weigh 4 to 5.1 pounds. They soar high in courtship, often calling a fluting, "Hu-opp, hu-o-hu-opp" when near the nest. The egg is incubated for 47 days. The young fly by 75 days of age. This species is decreasing in number.

Feather-toed Hawk-eagle—*See* Mountain Hawk-eagle.

FISH AND SEA EAGLES

This group of 3.5- to 19.5-pound eagles is found throughout the world, except in South America. They inhabit forested shores of oceans, rivers, or lakes from the Arctic Circle to the Tropics. Their wings are long and broad; their tails are short and rounded, or wedge-shaped. Their short, scaly legs have powerful toes with long, sharp talons. Most fish eagles are brown or brown and white. Juveniles are brown, but hatchlings may be gray, brown, or white. Fish eagles frequently pirate food. They usually lay two, but occasionally one or three, white eggs that are 2 to 3.25 inches long. Their nests are 3 to 8 feet across and 1 to 12 feet deep, and are built in trees or on cliffs and reused for many years. Some of these eagles perform spectacular courtship rituals.

The three genera of fish and sea eagles are *Gypohierax, Haliaeetus,* and *Ichthyophaga.* There are eleven species of fish and sea eagles.

Golden Eagle

(Aquila chrysaetos) This booted eagle is probably the most numerous large eagle, and one of the best known. It lives on wooded and barren mountains throughout North America, Europe, Asia, and northern Africa. Adults are plain brown with amber-tipped nape feathers; juveniles are a darker brown. Depending on its habitat, this eagle ranges in weight from 7 to 13 pounds and in length from 30 to 36 inches. The female is up to one-third larger than the male. Golden Eagles eat mammals, large birds, and carrion. Their courtship ritual is a series of undulating dives, performed alone or in pairs. Their two freckled eggs are incubated for 40 to 45 days. The young fly by 70 days after hatching. Although small populations have disappeared from the eastern United States, these eagles are still abundant in the West. They have completely vanished from all the British Isles except Scotland.

Gray-headed Fishing Eagle

(Ichthyophaga ichthyaetus) This brown, white, and gray eagle is one of the smallest of the fish eagles. Males weigh 3.5 pounds; females weigh 5 to 6 pounds. It eats fish and lives near the quiet streams, lagoons, and lakes of tropical southern Asia. It is very noisy during courtship, shouting a loud, gurgling, "Awh-awhr." It usually lays two eggs, but occasionally lays four.

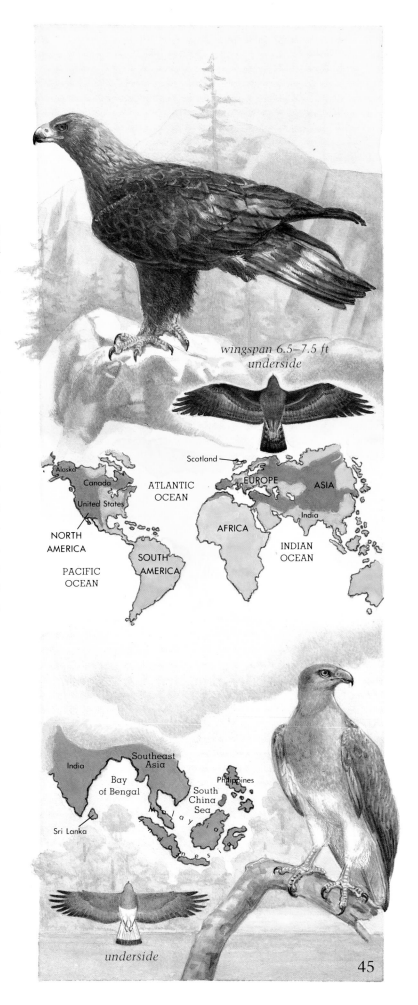

wingspan 6.5–7.5 ft
underside

underside

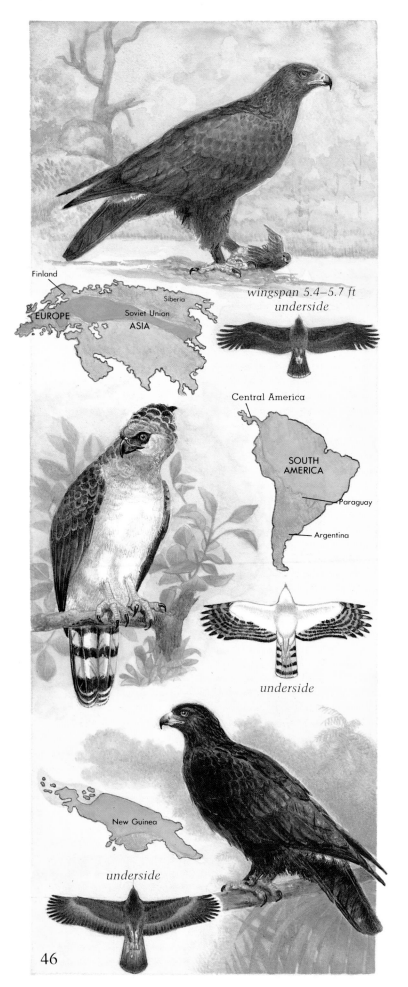

Finland
EUROPE
Siberia
Soviet Union
ASIA

wingspan 5.4–5.7 ft
underside

Central America
SOUTH AMERICA
Paraguay
Argentina

underside

New Guinea

underside

46

Greater Spotted Eagle

(Aquila clanga) This 27-inch booted eagle lives in swamps and deciduous woodlands from Finland in Europe to Siberia in the USSR. It migrates to southern Europe and northeastern Africa in winter. Males weigh 3.4 to 4.4 pounds; females weigh 4.7 to 7 pounds. Adults are dark brown; juveniles are darker and have large white spots. It eats small mammals, frogs, birds, and insects. In courtship it dives and soars, barking a shrill, "Tyuck-tyuck." Its two grayish white eggs are incubated for about 44 days. Its young fly by 65 days after hatching.

Guiana Crested Eagle

(Morphnus guianensis) This 26- to 30-inch harpy eagle weighs nearly 4 pounds and has an impressive crest. Adults are black and white; juveniles are heavily barred. It lives in thick, tropical jungles of Central and South America from Honduras to northern Paraguay and Argentina. It eats small monkeys, birds, and reptiles. It frequently perches in the highest tree for hours at a time. Its call is a loud, hoarse, three-syllabled whistle followed by a prolonged scream. Its cream-colored egg has brown spots.

Gurney's Eagle

(Aquila gurneyi) This black and chocolate-colored booted eagle is very rare and one of the least studied. It is 30 inches long and weighs 6.7 pounds. Juveniles are dark brown and cream or buff. It lives in the tropical forests along the coast of New Guinea, an island north of Australia.

Harpy Eagle

(Harpia harpyja) The name of this eagle means *witchlike*, because its crest gives it a witchlike look. This black, white, and gray harpy eagle is the largest and most powerful of all eagles. It is 32 to 36 inches long. Males weigh 9 to 10 pounds; females weigh up to 20 pounds. It has very short, broad wings that allow it to fly easily in dense, tropical jungles of southern Mexico and northeastern South America. Usually silent, it is seldom seen, except when soaring and uttering a loud, wailing, "Wheeeeoooooo," during courtship. It eats birds and tree-dwelling mammals such as monkeys, sloths, and opossums. The destruction of jungles threatens this eagle's survival.

HARPY OR BUTEONINE EAGLES

This small group of huge, powerful eagles includes the largest of all eagles. Harpy eagles range from 24 to 36 inches long and weigh from 3.5 to 20 pounds. These little-known and strikingly colored eagles live in tropical forests of South America, Mexico, the Philippines, and New Guinea, an island in the South Pacific. All have crests and many have short, broad wings for greater maneuverability among the trees. They eat large mammals, including monkeys. They build huge nests in tall trees and lay one to two white eggs. Juveniles are usually brown and white.

The five genera of harpy eagles are *Harpia, Harpyhaliaetus, Harpyopsis, Morphnus,* and *Pithecophaga.* There are six species of harpy eagles.

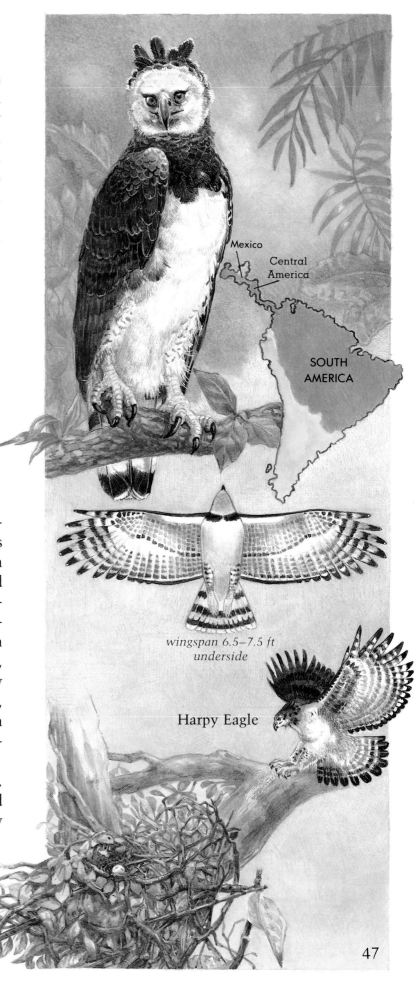

Mexico

Central America

SOUTH AMERICA

wingspan 6.5–7.5 ft underside

Harpy Eagle

Imperial Eagle

(Aquila heliaca) This 28- to 33-inch, brown booted eagle is similar to, but smaller than, the Golden Eagle. It has white patches on the nape and shoulders. Juveniles are tawny with dark brown streaks. Males weigh 5.7 to 8.7 pounds; females weigh 6 to 9.35 pounds. They live in subtropical woodlands and plains from Spain, where they are endangered, to Mongolia and East Africa. They eat small mammals, birds, reptiles, and carrion. Their mating display consists of soaring and a deep, barking, "Owk-owk." Their two to three eggs are incubated for about 43 days and young fly by 60 days of age.

wingspan 6.2–6.7 ft
underside

underside

Indian Black Eagle

(Ictinaetus malayensis) This little-known booted eagle is rather large, but lightly built. It is almost as large as a Bald Eagle. Adults are black. Juveniles are dark brown and buff streaked with white and black. It lives in the mountainous woodlands of southeast Asia from India to Malaysia. It eats small mammals, young birds, and eggs snatched from treetops. It is usually silent but utters a shrill cry during courtship both perched and on the wing. In its aerial mating display, it plunges thousands of feet. Its single egg is white splotched with brown, or pink splotched with dark red.

Isidor's Eagle

(Oroaetus isidori) Also called Black and Chestnut Eagle. Little is known about this 25- to 29-inch booted eagle. It lives on high subtropical slopes of the Andes Mountains in South America, from Argentina to Venezuela. It eats squirrels and monkeys. Adults are black and chestnut and have a large cardinal-like crest; juveniles are heavily streaked with buff. While gliding low over treetops, this eagle occasionally calls, "Chee-chee-chee." Its single egg is spotted. Its young fly about 120 days after hatching.

Java Hawk-eagle

(Spizaetus bartelsi) Very little is known about this 20- to 22-inch booted eagle. It is seldom seen. Adults are dark brown and have long crests. Juveniles are brown on top and dirty white underneath. This eagle may be closely related to Wallace's Hawk-eagle.

Lesser Fishing Eagle

(Ichthyophaga nana) This little fish eagle is very quiet and rarely seen. It is similar to, but smaller than, the Gray-headed Fishing Eagle. Adults are brown, white, and black; juveniles are paler. It lives in forested areas of India and Asia and in parts of Indonesia near fast-flowing, freshwater streams. It eats only fish.

underside

underside

underside

Lesser Spotted Eagle

(Aquila pomarina) This small, slim booted eagle is 24 to 26 inches long and weighs 2.5 to 4.75 pounds. It is quite common in the woodlands of central and eastern Europe, Greece, and India. It migrates to southeastern Africa in winter. Adults are brown and white; juveniles are darker. They eat small mammals, young birds, lizards, and large insects. During the mating display they make short, steep undulations while calling, "Kyek-kyek," in a high-pitched yap. Their one to three spotted eggs are incubated for about 45 days. Their young fly by 55 days after hatching.

wingspan 4.7–5.2 ft
underside

ASIA
Black
Sea
EUROPE
Greece
Caspian
Sea
Mediterranean
Sea
AFRICA
Arabian
Peninsula
India

Little Eagle

(Hieraaetus morphnoides) This small, robust booted eagle is 16 to 19 inches long and weighs 2 to 2.5 pounds. It is beautifully marked in shades of brown. Juveniles are mostly dark red-brown. It lives in Australia and New Guinea, an island north of Australia. It eats small mammals and young birds. During its undulating courtship displays, it drops as much as 200 feet. It constantly whistles, "Chew-chew-chew-chew-choo-oo-oo-oo-oo," starting slowly, ending rapidly, and falling in pitch. It lays one to two bluish eggs. Its young fly about 50 days after hatching.

New Guinea

wingspan 3+ ft

AUSTRALIA

underside, dark phase

underside, light phase

Long-crested Eagle

(Lophaetus occipitalis) This small booted eagle is 18.5 to 21 inches long and weighs 2 to 3.3 pounds. Adults are black or very dark brown with white wing patches and have impressive crests of long floppy plumes. Juveniles resemble adults but have smaller crests and white tips on the neck feathers. They live in both wooded and open country of tropical Africa. They eat small rodents and sometimes disabled birds. This noisy bird soars in display, repeatedly calling, "Keeeee-ee-eh" in a high-pitched scream. Its two grayish eggs are incubated for about 42 days. Its young fly by 65 days after hatching.

Madagascar Fish Eagle

(Haliaeetus vociferoides) This large, brown-and-white fish eagle is seldom seen because it lives in the deep forests of Madagascar, an island off the east coast of Africa. It feeds on fish that has washed ashore. It soars during courtship, calling a loud, eerie, "Quay-quay" or "Hoai-hoai."

Madagascar Serpent Eagle

(Eutriorchis astur) This rare, 22.5-inch snake eagle is brown and white and heavily barred. It lives only in the thick rain forests of Madagascar but has not been seen in recent years. It may be close to extinction, if not already extinct.

Martial Eagle

(Polemaetus bellicosus) This agressive booted eagle is the largest eagle in Africa. It is 26 to 30 inches long. Males weigh 11 pounds, females 13 to 13.5 pounds. Adults are gray-brown and white. Juveniles are dark gray and white. This eagle lives in the open country and lightly forested areas of tropical and southern Africa. It spends much time in the air on its huge 8.5-foot wings. It eats large birds, hyraxes, and dik-diks. It is silent, except when courting. Then it soars, calling, "Klee-klee-klee-klee-klooee-kloeeee-kuleee." Its single white or greenish blue egg is incubated for about 50 days and its young fly by 100 days after hatching.

AFRICA

wingspan 6.5–8.5 ft
underside

Mountain Hawk-eagle

(Spizaetus nipalensis) Also called Feather-toed Hawk-eagle. This large, powerful booted eagle is 24.5 to 28 inches long. It is brown and cinnamon colored, heavily barred, and has a long, pointed crest. Juveniles are largely white. Males weigh 5.5 pounds; females weigh about 8 pounds. These eagles are noisy but seldom seen. They live in the forests of southern Asia. They eat small mammals and large game birds. They soar and undulate when courting, giving a high, rapid bubbling trill. Their single egg may be pale gray, pink, or white blotched with red. The young fly about 80 days after the eggs are laid.

China
Taiwan
Hainan
Southeast Asia
India
Bay of Bengal
Sri Lanka

underside

New Guinea Harpy Eagle

(Harpyopsis novaeguineae) This 31-inch, gray-brown and white harpy eagle has a wingspan of 62 inches. It lives only in the lower mountain forests of New Guinea, a South Pacific island. It probably eats ground wallabies and piglets. Its call is an unpleasant, high-pitched, short, vibrant cry. Its survival is threatened by destruction of the forests.

Nicobar Serpent Eagle

(Spilornis klossi) Little is known about this small, brown-and-white snake eagle. It lives only in the tropical jungles of Great Nicobar Island near the northern tip of Sumatra. It is closely related to, and is probably similar to, the Crested Serpent Eagle. It is 17 to 18.5 inches long.

Ornate Hawk-eagle

(Spizaetus ornatus) This long-crested 21- to 25-inch booted eagle is one of the least known of the South American eagles. It lives in the tropical forests of Mexico, Central America, and South America. Adults are strikingly colored. Juveniles are mostly white with brown backs. Males weigh about 2 pounds; females weigh 3 to 3.5 pounds. They eat large ground birds and mammals. Pairs soar together in courtship, performing spirals and plunges. The call is a clear, thin, high-pitched scream, "Wheeoo-whee pee pee."

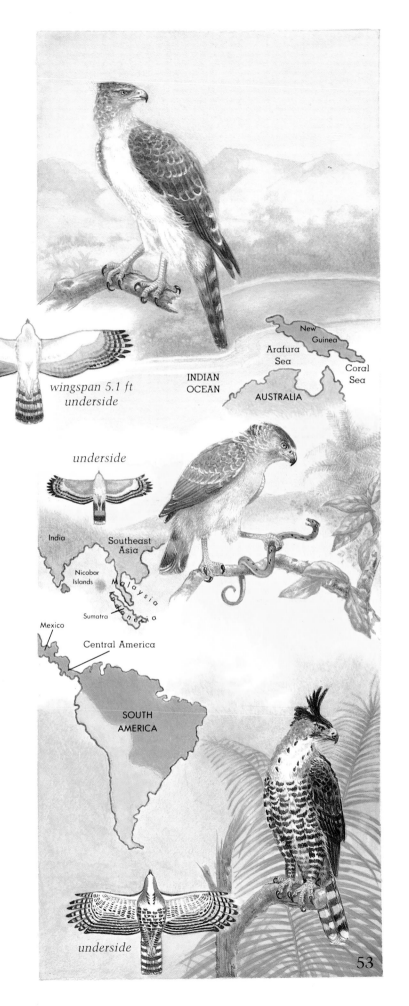

wingspan 5.1 ft
underside

underside

New Guinea
Arafura Sea
Coral Sea
INDIAN OCEAN
AUSTRALIA

India
Southeast Asia
Nicobar Islands
Malaysia
Indonesia
Sumatra
Mexico
Central America
SOUTH AMERICA

underside

53

Caspian Sea

Soviet Union

ASIA Mongolia

China

India

wingspan 7–8 ft
underside

PACIFIC OCEAN

South China Sea

Philippines

Borneo

Sulawesi

underside

Pallas' Sea Eagle

(Haliaeetus leucoryphus) In spite of its name, this brown fish eagle is seldom found near seacoasts. It lives along inland waterways of central Asia, migrating to the Caspian Sea in southwestern Russia in winter. Males of this golden-headed species weigh 5.8 to 7 pounds; females weigh 7.2 pounds. They will eat young ducks and storks but prefer dead fish or carrion. Pairs soar together in courtship. Their mating call is a deep, rich neigh. Their eggs are incubated for 35 days and their young fly about 70 days after hatching.

Palm-nut Eagle—*See* Vulturine Fish Eagle.

Philippine Eagle

(Pithecophaga jefferyi) This eagle was once known as the Philippine Monkey-eating Eagle. Its name was changed when it was discovered that it fed mostly on lemurs and other medium-size mammals and rarely on monkeys. It also eats hawks, lizards, and snakes. This 36-inch, brown-and-white harpy eagle is the second largest eagle and one of the world's rarest birds. Males weigh a little over 10 pounds; females are almost as large as a Harpy Eagle. They are found only in dense tropical forests on the large islands of the Philippines. They are usually silent but sometimes whistle a long, rather mellow, "Wheeew" while soaring during courtship. Their eggs are incubated for 60 days and their young fly 105 days after hatching. Almost extinct, this eagle is now protected by law.

Philippine Hawk-eagle

(Spizaetus philippensis) Practically nothing is known about this dark-brown and cinnamon-colored booted eagle. Juveniles are gray-brown and white. Adults are about 24 inches long. It lives in the tropical forests of the Philippines and is threatened by the destruction of its habitat.

Philippine Monkey-eating Eagle—*See* Philippine Eagle.

Philippine Serpent Eagle

(Spilornis holospilus) This beautifully marked, dark-brown and white snake eagle is very similar to the Crested Hawk-eagle and may be a subspecies of that eagle. It is fairly common in the tropical savannas and forests of the Philippines, but it has not been fully studied. It is 18 to 21.5 inches long. Its call is a series of short, far-ranging whistles followed by a cry of, "Pheeeeuw-pheeeeuw."

Rufous-bellied Eagle—*See* Chestnut-bellied Hawk-eagle.

Sandford's Sea Eagle

(Haliaeetus sandfordi) Little is known about this large, brown sea eagle. It is closely related to, and may be a subspecies of, the White-bellied Sea Eagle, but is colored differently. Its head is golden brown, and its belly is red-brown. Juveniles are speckled. It lives only on the Solomon Islands north of Australia and eats large birds, fish, and carrion.

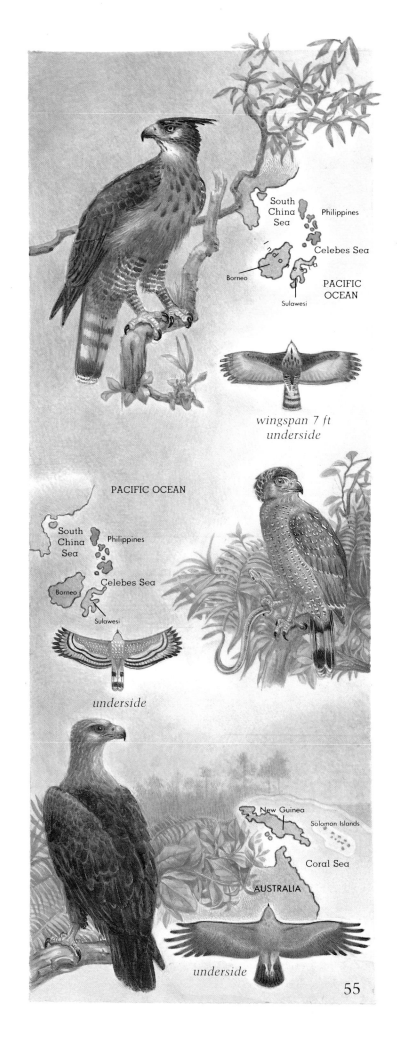

wingspan 7 ft
underside

underside

underside

European Snake Eagle

Serpent Eagle—*See* European Snake Eagle.

Short-toed Eagle—*See* European Snake Eagle.

SNAKE OR SERPENT EAGLES

This group of eagles may be closely related to kites. They probably evolved from kites about 500,000 years ago. Snake and serpent eagles have crested heads. Their rather short, strong, bare legs are covered with large, rough scales and end in short, powerful toes. These eagles are 17 to 27 inches long and weigh between 1.6 and 6.5 pounds. Hatchlings are usually white and juveniles are brown or brown and white. Snake eagles live in the tropical savannas and forests of Europe, Asia, Africa, and Australia. Little is known about many of the species. These reptile-eaters feed mostly on snakes, including some that are venomous. Using its beak, the eagle breaks a small snake's back, crushes its head, and then swallows it whole, headfirst. Venom is digested and does not harm the eagle. Snake eagles nest in tall trees. Their relatively small nests are 2 to 3 feet across and 8 to 10 inches deep. Their single egg is usually white.

The five genera of snake and serpent eagles are *Circaetus*, *Dryotriorchis*, *Eutriorchis*, *Spilornis*, and *Terathopius*. There are twelve species of snake and serpent eagles.

Smaller Banded Snake Eagle

(Circaetus cinerascens) This stumpy, 20- to 22-inch, heavily barred, gray-brown snake eagle spends most of its day perched in dead trees. It lives in well-wooded tropical savannas of Africa. It eats snakes, fish, frogs, and lizards. It rarely soars, but during courtship individuals or pairs circle high in the air calling a loud, clear, "Kok-kok-kok-kok-ko-ho." It is very secretive and is seldom seen.

Southern Banded Snake Eagle

(Circaetus fasciolatus) Little is known about this heavily barred, gray-brown and white snake eagle. It is 20 to 22 inches long. Males weigh about 2 pounds; females weigh about 2.4 pounds. It lives in the coastal woodlands of East Africa and eats snakes and lizards. During courtship, it calls a high-pitched, "Ko-ko-ko-ko-kaw," usually from a perch, but sometimes in flight.

Steller's Sea Eagle

(Haliaeetus pelagicus) This huge, dark-brown sea eagle is one of the world's most impressive birds and is the third largest eagle. It is 38 to 40 inches long. Males weigh 10 to 13 pounds; females weigh 15 to 18.75 pounds. It lives along rocky seashores and large rivers of northeastern Siberia, and winters in Japan and Korea. This eagle eats large fish, crabs, mollusks, waterfowl, young seals and other mammals, and carrion. During courtship it soars and emits a deep-toned bark, "Ra-ra-ra-rau-rau." Its eggs are incubated for 45 days and the young fly by 70 days after hatching.

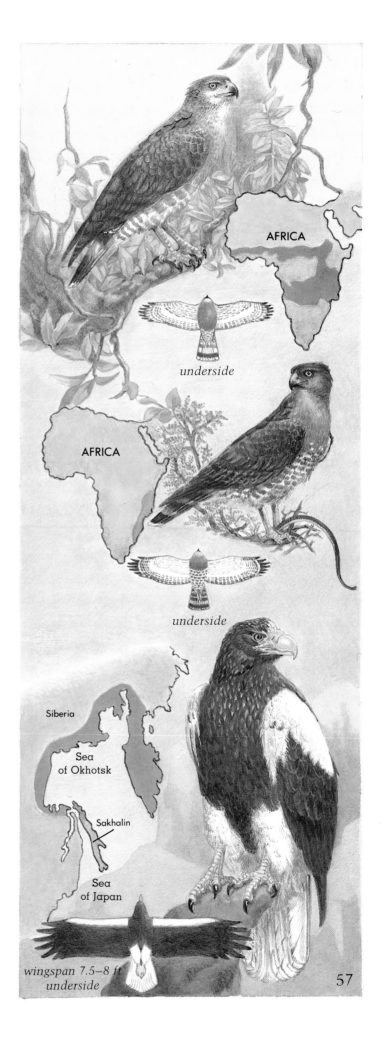

AFRICA

underside

AFRICA

underside

Siberia

Sea
of Okhotsk

Sakhalin

Sea
of Japan

wingspan 7.5–8 ft
underside

57

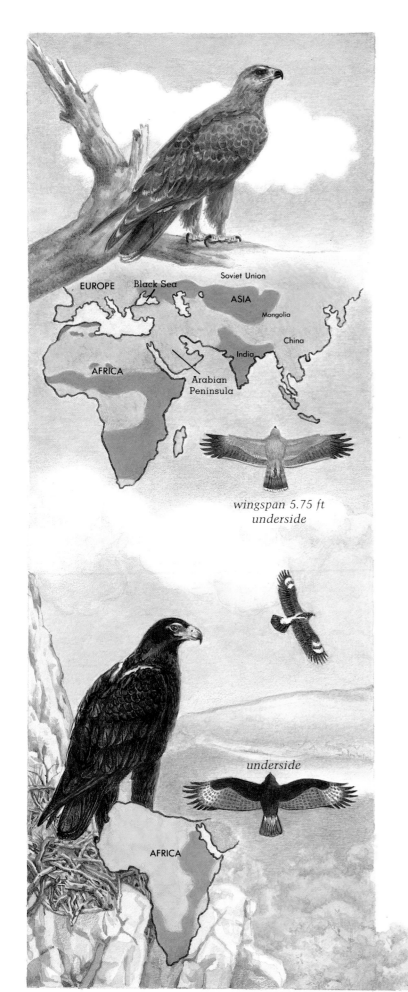

wingspan 5.75 ft
underside

underside

AFRICA

Steppe Eagle—*See* Tawny Eagle.

Tawny Eagle

(Aquila rapax) Also called Steppe Eagle. This booted eagle has many subspecies. Altogether, there are probably more Tawny Eagles than any other kind of eagle. They vary in color from dark to light red-brown. Most are reddish tawny brown. Juveniles are usually paler than adults and are often streaked. This eagle is 24 to 28 inches long. Males weigh 3.75 to 5 pounds; females weigh 4.2 to 6.5 pounds. They live in a variety of temperate and subtropical habitats, including deserts and woodlands of Africa and south central Europe and Asia from Greece to Mongolia. They eat almost anything but mostly carrion, mammals, termites, and ground birds. Males perform spectacular courtship displays. Their call is a barking, "Kowk-kowk." Females incubate their one to three white, sometimes spotted, eggs for about 45 days. The young fly by 55 days after hatching.

Verreaux's Eagle

(Aquila verreauxii) Also called Black Eagle. This large, powerful booted eagle is 28 to 32 inches long and weighs 7 to 12 pounds. It is coal black with white patches on the back, rump, and tail. Juveniles are ginger-brown and white streaked with brown. This eagle prefers the dry mountainous areas of Africa. It usually nests on cliffs. It eats hyraxes, dik-diks, and hares. Pairs perform spectacular, very swift, undulating courtship rituals, which may include cartwheels and pendulum swings. Their call is a whistling, "Heeee-oh." The two bluish white eggs are incubated for about 45 days. The young fly by 90 days after hatching.

Vulturine Fish Eagle

(*Gypohierax angolensis*) Also called Palm-nut Eagle. This 3- to 3.75 pound, white-and-black fish eagle is the only eagle that eats plant food. It eats the husks of oil palm nuts, dates, and other fruits, but also eats small fish, crabs, and frogs. It lives in forests and savannas of tropical Africa, where oil palm trees grow. In courtship it rolls and dives in pairs. It is usually silent but occasionally utters a low-pitched growl. Its single, heavily splotched egg is incubated for 44 days. The young fly within 90 days after hatching.

Wahlberg's Eagle

(*Aquila wahlbergi*) This slim booted eagle is one of the smallest eagles. It is 19 to 21 inches long. Males weigh 1 to 1.8 pounds; females weigh 1.5 to 3 pounds. Adults are dark brown. Juveniles look similar but have paler undersides. This eagle lives in tropical savannas of Africa, migrating from south to north in winter. It eats lizards, small mammals, and some game birds. Several pairs may perform mating rituals together, soaring very high and giving a shrill, whistling call, "Kleeeee-ay." The single egg is incubated for about 45 days. The young usually fly within 75 days of hatching.

Wallace's Hawk-eagle

(*Spizaetus nanus*) Little is known about this 18-inch booted eagle. It has a black back, heavily barred or streaked cinnamon-colored underparts, and a 2-inch crest of four or five black feathers. Juveniles are paler than adults with buff underparts. This eagle may weigh less than a pound. It lives in the tropical forests of Malaysia, Borneo, and Sumatra.

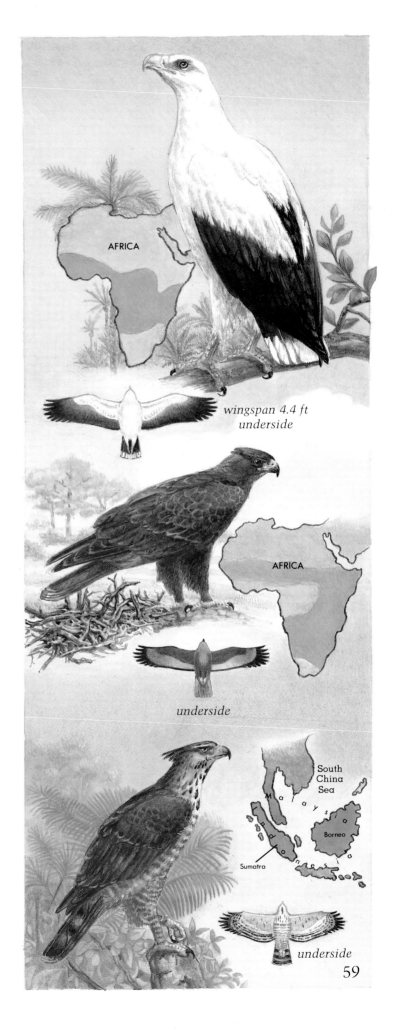

AFRICA

wingspan 4.4 ft
underside

AFRICA

underside

South China Sea

Borneo

Sumatra

underside

59

Wedge-tailed Eagle

(Aquila audax) This booted eagle is the largest bird of prey in Australia. It is 30 to 36 inches long, has a wingspan of more than 8 feet, and weighs from 5.5 to 10 pounds. It is brownish black with a tawny nape. Juveniles are dark brown with tawny red-brown heads and necks. These eagles live in dry savannas of Australia and the nearby island of Tasmania. They eat rabbits, hares, wallabies as big as themselves, and some carrion. In courtship, pairs soar together, the male swooping down at great speed and circling the female. The call is a shrill, "I see-I see." Their one to three eggs are light buff or white. Their young fly by 67 days after hatching.

wingspan 6.3–8+ ft
underside

White-bellied Sea Eagle

(Haliaeetus leucogaster) This brown-and-white eagle is the slimmest and most graceful of the fish and sea eagles. It weighs from 5.4 to 6.2 pounds. It lives along the coasts and major rivers of southern Asia and Australia. It eats fish and sea snakes. Pairs soar together during courtship, chasing, and looping the loop, while calling a ducklike quack. Their eggs are incubated for about 50 days. Their young fly by 70 days after hatching.

wingspan 5.8–7.15 ft
underside

White-tailed Sea Eagle

(Haliaeetus albicilla) Also called Erne, European Sea Eagle, and Gray Sea Eagle. This brown-and-white, 27- to 36-inch sea eagle is closely related to the Bald Eagle. Males weigh 6.7 to 11 pounds; females 8.3 to 14.4 pounds. It lives along rocky coasts, large rivers, and inland lakes of Greenland, Europe, and Asia. It eats fish, waterfowl, mammals, and carrion. In courtship, pairs soar together while calling in duet. The male's call is, "Krick-krick-krick-krick"; the female's is, "Ra-rack-rack-rack-rack." Sometimes the female turns on her back and presents her claws to the male. Its eggs are incubated for about 40 days. The young fly by 70 days after hatching.

Greenland

Iceland

Norway

Soviet Union

EUROPE ASIA

China Japan

India

wingspan 6.5–7.8 ft
underside

For Further Reading

Brown, Leslie. *Eagles of the World.* New York: Universe Books, 1976.

Brown, Leslie, and Amadon, D. *Eagles, Hawks & Falcons of the World.* Vols. 1 & 2. New York: McGraw-Hill Book Company, 1968.

Brown, Leslie; Urban, Emil K,; and Newman, Kenneth. *The Birds of Africa.* Vol. 1. New York: Academic Press, 1982.

Cowden, Jeanne. "Adventures with South Africa's Black Eagles." *National Geographic,* October 1968, pp. 533–543.

Craighead, John. "Sharing the Lives of Wild Golden Eagles." *National Geographic,* September 1967, pp. 420–439.

Dunstan, Thomas C. "Our Bald Eagle." *National Geographic,* February 1978, pp. 186–199.

Gonzalez Grande, Jose Luis. "Spain's Imperial Eagle." *Natural History,* January 1981, pp. 40–43.

Grossman, Mary Louise, and Hamlet, John. *Birds of Prey of the World.* New York: Clarkson N. Potter, Inc., 1964.

Harrison, Colin. *A Field Guide to the Nests, Eggs and Nestlings of British and European Birds.* London: William Collins Sons & Co. Ltd, 1975.

Johnson, Johnny. "The Garbage Eagles." *Natural History,* August 1983, pp. 43–45.

Kennedy, Robert S. "Saving the Philippine Eagle." *National Geographic,* June 1981, pp. 847–856.

McConoughey, Jana. *The Bald Eagle.* Mankato, Minnesota: Crestwood House, 1983.

Patent, Dorothy Hinshaw. *Where the Bald Eagles Gather.* New York: Clarion Books, 1984.

Pistorius, Alan. "Africa's Aerobatic Eagle: A High-Speed Tailless Glider." *Science Digest,* July 1985, pp. 45–49.

Riley, Terry. *Eagles and Other Hunters of the Sky.* London: Dean & Son Ltd., 1982.

Roever, J. M., and Roever, Wilfried. *The North American Eagles.* Austin, Texas: Steck-Vaughn Company, 1973.

Ryden, Hope. *America's Bald Eagle.* New York: G. P. Putnam's Sons, 1985.

Wexo, John Bennett. *Eagles/Zoobooks 2.* San Diego, California: Wildlife Education, Ltd., 1985.

Helen Roney Sattler is noted for her many fine nonfiction books for young readers. Among her highly praised, award-winning titles are *Hominids: A Look Back at Our Ancestors*; *Dinosaurs of North America*; *The Illustrated Dinosaur Dictionary*; *Baby Dinosaurs*; *Tyrannosaurus Rex and Its Kin*; *Pterosaurs, the Flying Reptiles*; *Sharks, the Super Fish*; *Whales, the Nomads of the Sea*; *Train Whistles*; and *Recipes for Art and Craft Materials.* Mrs. Sattler has been an elementary school teacher and a children's librarian. She lives in Bartlesville, Oklahoma.

Jean Day Zallinger has illustrated over fifty books for children, most of them on scientific subjects. In addition to her work as an illustrator, she taught illustration and drawing at Paier College of Art, which is near her home in Connecticut, for many years. A meticulous researcher, and noted for her careful attention to scientific detail, she worked for over two years to produce the watercolor paintings for *The Book of Eagles.* Her illustrations appear in three other books by Helen Roney Sattler, *Baby Dinosaurs*; *Sharks, the Super Fish*; and *Whales, the Nomads of the Sea.*